Body Language Secrets:
Optimum Performance

Other titles in this series
(all by Susan Quilliam):

Body Language Secrets: Making Love Work
Body Language Secrets: Success at Work
Body Language Secrets: Successful Social Life
Body Language Secrets: Total Strangers
Body Language Secrets: Babies and Children

Body Language Secrets: Optimum Performance

Susan Quilliam

Thorsons
An Imprint of HarperCollins*Publishers*

Thorsons
An Imprint of HarperCollins*Publishers*
77–85 Fulham Palace Road,
Hammersmith, London W6 8JB
1160 Battery Street,
San Francisco, California 94111-1213

Published by Thorsons 1996
10 9 8 7 6 5 4 3 2 1

© Transformation Management 1996

Susan Quilliam asserts the moral right to
be identified as the author of this work

A catalogue record for this book
is available from the British Library

ISBN 0 7225 3129 X

Printed in Great Britain by
Woolnough Bookbinding Limited, Irthlingborough

To Desmond Morris – who else?

Contents

Acknowledgements

I would first like to acknowledge the many sources and individuals who helped me gain my research material, particularly the staff of the Open University Library, the staff of the University of London Library, and Felicity Sinclair. A special acknowledgement to Samantha Smeraglia for her ability to collate my research so wonderfully!

My thanks also to: Barbara Levy, my agent, for her continued support; Sharon Scotland, the illustrator; to Jane Graham-Maw, Michele Turney, Jenni Maas and Barbara Vesey from

Thorsons for making the writing and
production of this book such an enjoyable
experience; to my personal assistant June
Bulley for her constant administrative
excellence.

A final thank you to my husband Ian who, as
always, makes all things possible.

Throughout this book, the people referred to
could be either 'he' or 'she'. Consistently
referring to one gender would not only raise
political issues, but would be unfair to the
'other kind'! In general, therefore, unless to do
otherwise would make the text inaccurate,
I have alternated pronouns in successive
questions in this book, to give a balanced feel.

Preface

Before you read this book, remember that body language:

- is every kind of human behaviour *except* the words spoken – from gestures to breathing, from the way muscles move to a person's use of time
- is not able to tell you everything – you may need the words too
- does not let you read everyone like a book – because everyone has his or her own personalized body language
- will not give you power over people – they will not respond unless they want to

- will not work if you try to change others
  – you can only ever shift what *you* do and
  alter the situation that way
- is about gathering information – you will
  be more successful if you do
- is something you already know – your
  natural body language works best
- is best tried out slowly and carefully – new
  body language patterns can look false
- works by trial and error: do more of what
  succeeds, and stop doing anything that
  doesn't!

How Can Body Language Help Me Perform Better in My Life?

Body language is the foundation of personal performance. This is something we have realized only in the last few years, when psychologists have begun to understand the essential links between mind and body. For the way you use nonverbal communication reflects and affects the way you approach things in every area of your life.

Reading your own body language lets you understand your own mental and emotional tactics. You can start to interpret the way you think, how you remember, how you learn.

You can begin to analyse your own emotions, when you feel them, how you feel them – and what use they are to you. You can begin to trace how your body language reflects your personality – and how that affects the way people react to you.

You can also start to work *with* rather than *against* your own nonverbal patterns. And, doing so, you can often increase your effectiveness in a whole range of areas. Rather than simply ignoring or pushing down the signals from outside and inside your body, you can start to listen to those signals and use what they are telling you. Rather than getting annoyed when, for example, you are performing below par, you can let your body tell you how to solve the problem.

Also, body language can actually help you change. For one of the most exciting recent developments in psychology suggests that if, in certain situations, we alter our body language, we can also alter our attitudes, perceptions and emotions. It is true that where our minds go, our bodies can often follow; if we decide to do something, then our bodies will rise to the challenge. And it is also true that where our bodies go, our minds can often follow, and that if we act, then our thoughts and feelings will often fall into place too.

If you want to be really effective in life, you have to be aware of body language – and use it.

Does My Natural Physical Appearance Affect the Way People Relate to Me?

The answer to this question is a definite yes. Human beings are influenced by appearance; children as young as two or three months old consistently look, gurgle and smile at photos of some faces more than others.

So what particular elements influence most? Being tall and slim will influence people in your favour; they are likely to judge you as more competent and more attractive. If you are male, being too thin may mean you are seen as a wimp, while fat people of both genders are judged as lazy and self-indulgent.

Do you seem 'all woman' or 'all man'? Very obvious gender signals, such as big breasts and buttocks on a female, or wide shoulders and small buttocks on a male, can make you seem more alluring in situations where sexual attraction is important, such as at a disco. Where sex is not as relevant, though, such as at work, such features can make people mistrust you, judge you as less intelligent, or think you are 'only after one thing'.

When it comes to the shape of your face, the more 'babyish' your face looks the more people will warm to you. Recent research at the University of St Andrews has shown that so-called 'infantile signals' – small nose, full lips, huge eyes, small chin and high cheekbones – stir up people's protective instincts. But these signals may also mean that people do not take you seriously. More mature features, such as a large nose or a prominent jaw, may well make people see you as more of an equal, and be more impressed by what you say or do – even if they do not feel quite so friendly towards you.

Colouring also counts. Sadly, skin colour makes you likely to be stereotyped, sometimes making people prejudge how intelligent you are, how likely you are to succeed in career terms – or how likely you are to break the law! Hair colour can also be seen as reflection of personality: blondes of both genders are seen both as 'more fun' and less intelligent, while redheads are traditionally thought to have fiery tempers, and brunettes to be serious and introverted.

Grey hair can be seen as a sign of distinguished elegance in men, though because it shows that a woman is old enough to be past her childbearing years, it is regarded as less appealing in a woman. (Hence the existence of over ten 'grey hair colouring' products for women currently on the market in Britain, against one equivalent product for men!)

All this can seem very depressing. People make an initial judgement in the first ten seconds of meeting you – and base that judgement on your appearance. And it may seem as if you cannot argue with that.

In fact, things are not as bad as they seem. Not only can some parts of 'natural' appearance be shifted – through exercise, careful dressing and 'the appliance of science' – research has also shown that when people see the wider range of body language that expresses your personality, they can very easily revise their initial judgment. Given ten hours instead of ten seconds, you can influence and attract, whatever your natural appearance.

How Can I Dress for Success?

What kind of success do you want? Everything you wear – clothes, hairstyle, jewellery, accessories – makes a nonverbal statement about your income, your status, your occupation, your personality, your age and your motives. But whether these statements mean that you succeed or fail depends very much on what game you want to play.

Do you want dress for success at work? Then you need to discover what the 'career uniform' is. This does not only mean following the rules in professions such as the army or catering

trade, where an actual uniform is worn. What it means is being aware of the style that has spontaneously developed within your company. Are suits in? Are perms out? How brightly coloured are the ties people wear? Because human beings feel more comfortable with others who 'copy' rather than buck the trend, following the company style consensus may mean all the difference between being simply tolerated and actively promoted.

Do you want to make friends? Ask first who these friends are and then what statement they make about themselves by what they wear. If the statement is 'income' or 'status', then you may need to dress expensively. But if your friends are those who do not have wealth or who do not value it, success may well be down to the creative and quirky use of low-cost materials. And if the people you mix with like to be seen as 'practical', spending more time on their families than on fashion, for example, then to be accepted you may have to wear down-to-earth rather than stylish clothes.

Success in love is often thought to depend on dressing sexily. Men, for example, tend to believe that if people dress to show off the more sexual parts of their anatomy, then what they want is sex. But this is not necessarily true for women, who may dress sexily to feel attractive, and sometimes to score points off their female rivals – but very rarely to signal that they simply want sex.

In fact, success guidelines in this context are these: To attract a partner initially, wear what gets his or her attention – that way, you are more likely to make contact and get talking. Women tend to be attracted to people who are fashionable and colour-co-ordinated, while men notice strong colours and shape-enhancing styles. Once you have attracted your partner, and got to know him or her, then choose your clothes first to reflect those parts of your personality that he or she particularly likes – your sense of fun, your elegance, your practicality – and secondly to encourage your partner literally to keep in contact with you because you wear sensuous, touchable clothes!

The bottom line, with all dress decisions, is to fit the time, the place, the context and the people. The more you understand about whomever you are dressing to impress – and the more you use that understanding to customize what you wear – the more successful you will be.

How Does My Environment Reflect What I Am Like as a Person?

If your environment truly reflects you – in other words, if you have actually chosen what is in it – then it will show other people a great deal about you.

For example, how introverted or extroverted are you? Studies show that physiologically, extroverts are better able to cope with sensory stimulation than are introverts. It is likely, then, that if you are the former you will fill your environment with rich colours and patterns and a great deal of detail in design; if you are the latter, you will opt for simple shapes, plain colours, dim lighting. Of course, you may be more or less introverted or extroverted in different situations, so you may allow more colour and detail in the public areas of your life such as the kitchen or the hall, and quieter design in the more private areas such as the bedroom.

Here is another personality distinction: Which of your three major senses is most important to you – sight, hearing or touch? For every human has a preferred sense – one which, almost from the beginning of our lives, is the one that attracts us most. Our preference then influences the way we arrange our environment. If you are a 'visual' person then you are likely to put the emphasis on how things look – as did one top designer who bought his easy chairs solely for their appearance, and realized only after they had

been delivered that they were excruciatingly
uncomfortable to sit on!

What if you are a person to whom sounds or
voices matter most? Your money will go on
the stereo system and you may never even get
round to repainting the walls or replacing
battered or unfashionable furniture. If you are
a person to whom touch is vital, then you will
spend most time and money on deep,
luxurious seating and velvet cushions. In fact,
most people combine all three senses in
varying amounts and contexts; consider what
the balance is for you.

What is the main focus of your environment?
If people are the most important thing in your
world, then your environment will probably
reflect that. The furniture focus will be
'social', with chairs and sofas turned towards

each other; a round or oval table where you can easily see people and interact with them; a soft sofa where you can cuddle up.

What if your space is centred around something neutral, perhaps a log fire? This does not mean that people are unimportant to you. It may mean, however, that you need to focus inside yourself, need time and space for yourself when you get home. If your focus is outward, perhaps a chair placed by a window, then you like to make contact with the outside world; perhaps you do not go out much during the day, or that even if you do you still see what happens 'out there' as vital.

A final thought: If you feel uneasy in your surroundings it could be because they do not truly reflect who you are. Try adding elements, or taking them away, using the insights above as a guideline. Consciously designing your environment to reflect your personality can make you feel more at home.

What Do I See in My 'Mind's Eye'?

If you have seen something once, then you can imagine it. Even if you have never seen something, given a good enough description or enough similar experiences, you can think of what it would look like.

When you do this, you use your 'mind's eye'. You conjure up a picture of what you are thinking about. So if asked to think of your kitchen at home, then you will almost certainly visualize that room. Every human being can do this – even if some of us are less able to remember their mental pictures than are others.

The study of this part of body language – the pictures people have inside their heads – is a new and very interesting development in the field of psychology. One of the things such study has shown is that what you see in your mind's eye is never the same as reality. Even if you think of something you know well, such as your kitchen sink, you will not see it in your mind's eye as you would in real life. In your mind's eye you might see that sink much more vaguely than it really is; perhaps not as brightly coloured; smaller or bigger than in reality. You might see it as full of water, empty of water, stacked with dishes – or with someone standing by it. The same kitchen sink as visualized by different people looks very different.

Fascinatingly, it now seems that these differences are linked to our emotions. We see differently in our mind's eye things that we feel differently about. Everyone has his (or her) own special way of seeing things – but, for example, some people actually flood their mind's eye image with a warm pinkish tinge when they feel very optimistic about something. On the other hand, if pessimistic or depressed, some people 'add' a cold bluish tint to what they imagine. So phrases like 'rose-coloured glasses ... I'm feeling blue ...' are not just words; they describe the way that some of us, at least, actually visualize things.

It is not only colour that reflects what we feel. Shape, brightness, focus, contrast, movement – all these vary in our mind's eye, and each variation reflects how we think and feel about what we see. Photographers and cameramen know all about this – and often manipulate their images to create feelings in the same way that the human brain does. If we are in love, for example, we often imagine our partner's face as slightly softened; in the same way, wedding photographers will use soft focus for the shot of the bride and groom. If we are scared of people, however small they actually are in real life, we often see them in our mind's eye as looming above us; film-makers copy this when they shoot from below to communicate a feeling of fear to the viewer.

Studying the mind's eye is something new. But already it is beginning to look possible that we can use it to help people in various ways – with phobias, with traumas, with all kinds of personal development issues. Changing the way we see things – through our mind's eye – may well prove to be one of the keys to enabling human beings to live life to the full.

How Do My Gestures Show Me How My Mind Works?

What you think in your mind, you reflect in your gestures. As you talk, so you trace in the air what you experience in your mind's eye and your 'mind's ear' – a 'between the lines' glimpse of what your words are not saying.

Your gestures might reflect reality. You might draw out in the air something you have seen or heard – to communicate it to others. Of course gestures never literally nor accurately depict the size and shape, rhythm, volume or sensation of what you have experienced. But they do show how your mind works on these experiences – they do show how you think about them.

So let's say you use the classic angler's gesture that goes with the words 'it was *that* big.' That gesture does not reveal the actual size of the fish – but it does show the size you would really want it to be. A series of tense circular hand movements as you describe how your car would not start does not mimic accurately the sound of the failing ignition. But it does reflect both the rhythm of that sound and the frustration you felt when you heard it!

Gestures also reflect more abstract things. You talk about a friendship and curve your hands together tightly. You describe a project you are starting and wave your hands vaguely. You say you are signing contracts on a new house, and slap one fist into the other hand's

open palm. Here, you are revealing how you think about concepts – a friendship, a project, a house purchase. And again, the gestures (taken in context) let observers read between the lines. The tight circle shows that you believe you and your friend are close. The unclear shapes show the project that you are working on is vague or undeveloped. The forceful fist gesture shows your excitement about buying a house.

Because everyone's mind works differently, the same gestures have different meanings for different people. But there are some general guidelines that may help you interpret. For instance, the size of your gestures often indicates how important the thing is that you are talking about – a big gesture indicating that something is vital, a small gesture that it is trivial. A moving gesture can show progression – how something is developing or evolving. Speed in a gesture is often linked to positive or negative emotion – slow gestures expressing gentleness or boredom, fast gestures revealing excitement or tension.

Two hands used for the same movement emphasizes what you are talking about – you use both hands to make the point more unmistakably than if you used just one. But each of your hands, acting independently, can also 'act out' elements in what you are saying. The relative position of each hand can then indicate the relationship of the things you are talking about – as in the friendship gesture described earlier.

Where are your gestures positioned around you? A 'high' gesture, above shoulder level, may indicate status, significance or positivity.

If your hands touch your body then they are indicating physical or emotional closeness. If they move away from your body, they indicate distance – worry if you catch yourself talking about someone who is supposed to be close to you but find yourself using away-from-the-body gestures!

What shapes do your hands make as they move? Flat, closed hands indicate straight, direct concepts – certainty, concentration, clarity. If moving downwards, they can indicate an ending or a halt; if turned upwards, openness or a question; if pointed forwards, a forward move. Hands with fingers open often reveal uncertainty or vagueness. Finally, hands that are curved, whether apart or together, tend to show positive emotions or ideas – support, affection, closeness, unity, completion.

How Does My Body Help Me Remember Things?

Whenever we experience something, we also store that experience. In other words, we put sights, sounds and feelings into our physiological memory banks, then retrieve these memories. We cannot help remember everything we have ever done, because our experience is so vast and because our ability to recall things may fade with time. But we can remember a great deal. You can probably recall, for example, what colour your bathroom is, or how the bath water sounds rushing down the plughole.

And if you remind your body of a past memory, then it will give you that memory back. The images in a photo album will bring back tiny and very specific details of people and places we had long forgotten. A special tune can reduce us to tears because it reminds us of a particular face, a particular voice, a particular kiss. The smell as we enter a tiny, musty grocer's store may take us all the way back to the corner shop we used to visit as children.

Some counsellors go one stage further – they claim that if we place our bodies in positions of particular stress, for example by breathing deeply and rapidly for extended periods, then feelings that have been buried for years will come to the surface. And as we express those emotions – of anger, joy or fear – we may well be able to remember much more clearly the original events that made us feel those emotions, many decades ago. Once again, we are using our bodies directly to stir up old memories.

Recent research by U.S. psychologists Richard Bandler and John Grinder takes a new tack. They suggest that our eyes move in particular ways when we remember particular things. So, for example, if we are remembering something we have seen – a face, a house, a building – in our mind's eye, then we will look up and to the left (or right, if we are left-handed). If we are remembering something we have heard – a sound, a voice – in our mind's ear, then we will look across to the left (right if left-handed). And if we are remembering something we have felt – a hug from a friend, a moment of strong emotion – then we will look slightly down and to the right. Though

these movements are tiny and rapid, the
suggestion is that they are the body's way of
bringing to mind very specific memories.

How much can you use any of these methods
to help you remember things? It is certainly
worth trying all of them: using mementos to
help you reminisce over past events, working
with a counsellor who specializes in
'bodywork' to retrieve early emotional
memories, experimenting with looking in
different directions when trying to remember
something you have seen or heard. Of course,
none of these approaches is guaranteed. But it
is beginning to become clear that, using body
language as a lever, we may be able to
remember far more than we ever thought we
could.

How Can I Spell Better?

Are you hopeless with words? If it is true that when you remember things you have seen, your eyes move in a particular way (*see page 45*), then this can help you develop your ability to spell.

Robert Dilts, a student of the original researchers who made the link between memory and eye position, went on to study the body language differences between people who spell well in the English language, and people who do not spell well.

Dilts found some interesting things. When asked to remember a word, the 'good spellers' consistently glanced up and to the left (right for left-handed people). Some of them even lifted their heads, as if to 'get a better view'. And they actually reported being able to 'see' the word they were spelling in their mind's eye – very often in white lettering on a black background, as if they were actually remembering the very chalkboard on which they had first seen the word spelled!

Poor spellers, on the other hand, could not mentally see the word at all. They had no picture in their mind's eye, and just guessed at what the spelling was before finally getting it wrong. They also did not look up, but kept their heads down, looking at the floor while trying to spell.

Dilts tried an unusual experiment – one which he has successfully repeated with many people since. He asked the poor spellers to look at a word on a piece of paper; then he asked them to try to recall the word while using the body language of good spellers. Amazingly, with a change of posture and eye direction, these people could often see their chosen word, and spell it correctly – and could repeat that success in future.

Try repeating Dilts' experiment. First, write down a word you know you can spell. Then imagine it on a board, floating above your head and a little to your left (right, if you are left-handed). Can you see the board clearly? Can you see the word on the board? If not, imagine it bigger and brighter, until each letter is obvious. Then 'read' out the word, letter by letter, forwards then backwards

– just to be sure you have all the letters in place.

Once you can do this, try putting a more difficult word 'on the board'. Once you are sitting up and looking up, make the word as big and bright as you need to in order to see it. Keep going until you can read the word letter by letter, forwards and backwards. Practise perhaps 20 times, to hammer it home. On the next occasion you need to spell that word, use the right body language – sitting up and looking up.

Then, whenever you see a word you know you are not sure of, pop it up on your board. Make it big and bright, practise reading it forwards and backwards – until you know that you will get it right in the future.

What Does Body Language Reveal About My Idea of Time?

Everybody has an image in his (or her) mind's eye of how he sees the past or the future. It is developed as you grow, by seeing clocks, calendars, diaries and other ways of 'marking time'. It means that when you are asked what happened on a particular day in the past, you often get a mental representation of it. And if you are asked to imagine what you will be doing on a particular day in the future, you are often able to visualize the date you are thinking about.

Research carried out in the U.S. suggests that, fascinatingly, most people see this mental image of events in the past and future as actually being in a specific position, in space, in relation to their bodies. The past is usually over to the left or slightly behind us; the future is often over to the right or in front. Past and future are usually 'joined' by an imaginary line, which would seem to run directly through our bodies. In fact, we often reflect what we see in our mind's eye by phrases such as 'I'm putting the past behind me,' 'here and now' or 'the future lies ahead ...'

In terms of body language, people actually signal the way they 'see' time – by the way they gesture and the direction in which they look. If, when you think of what happened last Christmas you see that as to your left and slightly behind you, then as you talk about it you will also tend to look back to your left, and make a minute hand-movement in that direction.

If, when you imagine what will happen on your next birthday, you see that as in front of you, then when you talk about your upcoming birthday party your hand-movements will tend to point forward and you will face forward. Not surprisingly, when you discuss the present you are likely to make gestures that indicate the spot you are standing on.

And if you are talking about something that has happened in the past and will go on happening in the future, your gestures and the direction in which you look may well trace your imaginary 'time' line, from past to future, from left to right or from back to front. Your time line will have a particular shape: some time lines are simply straight, others curve or go in waves.

Your time-line shape can also alter according to how you feel about the events on it. So, for example, pay attention if you see yourself tracing a downward sloping time line with your hand as you describe how you see your life developing; you are probably feeling pessimistic about some aspect of it. On the other hand, if you use an upward time-line movement, the chances are that your mood is an optimistic one – you see the future actually stretching ... 'onwards and upwards ...'

How Does My Body Learn Naturally?

Desmond Morris, who first brought nonverbal communication to the attention of the Western world, once wrote that a human being, the naked ape '... is a teaching ape'. Almost more miraculously, however, the naked ape is a learning ape. Unlike most mammals, and far more than our primate cousins, we learn from what we see around us, through imitation.

This ability is innate and instinctive. As early as a few minutes after birth, newborns are able to copy vital survival movements such as

opening their mouths (to take food) and
sticking out their tongues (to refuse food).
And most of us are very well aware that
children learn by copying – not only the things
we want them to imitate, such as eating with a
knife and fork, but also the things we do *not*
want them to imitate, like the swear word we
hear our three-year-old chanting happily to
herself! It is this innate ability to copy which
lets children develop so rapidly, and master so
many of the complex skills that make them
human, such as walking, talking, reading and
writing.

As adults, it may seem to us that we do not
learn in this way, but we do. Right up to the
time we die our bodies imitate what we see
around us. We copy the obvious bits of other
people's behaviour, such as posture, gesture
and facial expression, imitating someone else's

nonverbal patterns often within minutes of meeting. You may well have noticed how you 'pick up' a person's accent if you spend time with her (or him). But have you noticed how you copy her way of opening a door, her particular taste in food, her habit of sighing and leaning back in the chair at moments of deep satisfaction?

We also, amazingly, copy what happens to someone physiologically. So if someone we are close to gets irritated and her heart rate rises, her breathing quickens and adrenalin rushes round her body, then we will be similarly affected.

And if we spend a lot of time with this person, living or working with her regularly, then we may well learn to reproduce this reaction in a more generalized way. If something happens that would have irritated her, we will learn to get irritated ourselves – even if she is not in the room. In this way, we even 'learn' illness from other people, developing stomach ulcers, tension headaches or back problems simply because someone we are close to suffers from these conditions.

Happily, we also learn more positive nonverbal approaches. We can pick up other people's sense of humour, their tidiness, their love of nature. And of course, we lend them our talents in return. Because our bodies learn, we give and receive body language strategies every day of our lives.

What Happens When I Cannot Concentrate – and Is There Anything I Can Do About It?

Let's begin by looking at what happens when you *can* concentrate. You focus in on one thing. Your vision narrows, your hearing filters out what is not important. You reflect this in your body language by leaning forwards, staring at what interests you and raising your shoulders as if to block out everything else.

But what if you cannot concentrate? Then the outside world distracts you. One thing or another keeps shifting you away from a concentrated state. You glance around, turn around, get caught up in what you hear and see.

What can you do to concentrate better? If you are aware of the distraction, you can change it. But your body can be distracted by things that you may not be aware of. You may not register that the lighting is too dim, but your body may think it is time for sleep and so lose energy for what you are doing. You may not realize that silence may be distracting you, but too little sound can make your body wonder if something is wrong, and so be on the defensive instead of focused on the job in hand.

The distraction may not be outside, but inside you. There are many body functions that are so vital to survival that they take precedence over everything else. So if you have just eaten and need energy to digest your food, this may come first as far as your body is concerned; hard work after a meal just may not be possible. Equally, studies have shown that if your temperature rises or falls too much, if you are too hungry or thirsty, or if you have not had enough rest, your body will alert you to these potentially threatening conditions and keep on giving you these 'alert' messages until you take action.

And, unfortunately, your body can play tricks on you. If you are tense about doing a task your body may well provide you with an excuse not to do it by distracting you with a signal that seems like a survival issue. You suddenly feel very sleepy or very hungry, even if you are well rested and well fed! If this happens to you, rather than resting or eating try reducing any tension you may feel by stretching and breathing deeply. You may find that your fatigue or hunger has disappeared.

Lastly, give your concentration an extra boost by taking on the right body language. Literally turn your back on any possible distractions and focus your attention on the task in hand. Bend over your desk, hunch your shoulders, make your task the centre of your focus. If your body acts as if it is concentrating, then mysteriously you may soon find that your mind does too!

Does My Body Really Talk to Me?

Unbelievable as it may sound, your body communicates with you on a minute-by-minute basis. It tells you when to take action, when to avoid something, even when to be happy!

Actually, you already know this. You already know that your body communicates with you about survival issues. For example, if you are thirsty your body signals this by giving you a particular sensation in your mouth and throat. If you need sleep then your eyelids droop, your limbs feel heavy and you yawn. If your finger is too close to a candle flame then your body alerts you immediately, with a sharp pain that makes you pull your hand back. These physical sensations, these 'internal' signals, are an unmistakable message from your body that you cannot afford to ignore.

Your internal responses signal much more subtle things, too. They may tell you when you are going to be ill – migraine sufferers often report a 'warning feeling' a few days before the event. These responses may signal when you have made a mistake – as when you have a stomach upset and, mentally checking what might have caused it, you feel a sudden spasm as you think of one particular food. Your internal messages may even tell you what the weather's going to be like – as you will know very well if you are an arthritis sufferer who gets 'twinges' when rain is on the way.

Your body also signals, quite specifically, what your feelings about something are. If you experience any of the many emotions humans are capable of – such as fear, anger, anxiety, excitement, surprise, disgust – then what you experience are actual physical sensations inside your body. So if you are delighted that you have got something you wanted, that feeling of delight might be a light sensation throughout your body and a fluttering movement in your stomach. If you are upset that you have missed out on an opportunity, that feeling of sadness might take the form of a heavy sensation throughout your body and a prickling, tearful sensation in your eyes.

Take seriously the internal language of your body. It can tell you when you may have to be wary – perhaps your gut will churn or your back will tense up. It can tell you when you

might have reasons to be optimistic – perhaps
you will feel a smile coming on, or an excited
rise in your breathing rate. If you start to
become aware of the messages that your body
is sending you, you will be able to understand
situations more fully – because you will have
the evidence not only of your eyes and ears,
but also of how your body feels inside.

How Do I Tell When I Am Unsure About Something?

It is vital for you to know when you are sure about something and when not. Fascinatingly, human bodies do have a mechanism for expressing this – for telling you when you are uncertain and for signalling to others that you need support because of that uncertainty.

A simplified explanation of what happens is this. When your eyes, ears and other senses experience something and are sure of what they are experiencing, then they send clear messages to the brain via the nervous system. The brain interprets what it sees, and you take action.

But if your senses haven't enough information, or your brain cannot quite interpret that information or the information available is contradictory, then two things happen. First, you are alerted to lack of certainty by signals on the inside. Secondly, you send out signals of your lack of certainty on the outside – just in case you need others to help you.

Because what is happening to your body is focused around the nervous system, you are most likely to be aware of internal signals that are located around the central communication network of your nervous system, the spinal cord. Everyone's signals differ; yours might consist of a sinking feeling in your stomach, an uneasy feeling behind your eyes, a tension around your throat or a fluttering in your breathing. If the information you are working on is contradictory, then your body's signals may actually be different on one side than on the other, making you feel 'unbalanced'.

You will reflect all these internal signals on the outside of your body. You may shift to get rid of the discomfort in your stomach or head. You may rub your chest to ease your breathing. You may look puzzled or frown. If you feel 'unbalanced', you may find yourself shifting from one foot to the other, wiggling your shoulders, shaking your head or twisting your mouth. That verbal statement of uncertainty 'I'm weighing up the options' often has its parallel body language, a 'weighing' movement of the hands that seems to measure one thing against another.

Body language itself cannot make you any more sure of anything than you already are. No one movement or exercise will help if you simply do not have the facts at your fingertips, or if you need support to interpret those facts. Where body language *can* help is when you use it to alert you to your own uncertainty, when its signals hold you back from making a potential mistake in signing the document, making the promise, buying the car.

When you are sure, your nonverbal signals will alter. Your settled stomach, easy breathing, balanced posture, calm breathing or direct gaze will all tell you that, whether or not you are in fact making the correct judgment, you are at least certain about what you think and feel.

How Does My Body React to Danger?

When humans lived physically dangerous lives, those who did not know when to be afraid did not survive very long. So even though we now do not need to be on red alert for most of the day and night, we do react strongly to possible danger. We produce a set of body responses that we call fear – or anxiety, wariness, insecurity. Our bodies signal when something threatens – be it a physical threat such as a car speeding towards us or an emotional threat such as someone disliking us. We register these signals inside our bodies, and then display them on the outside, in order to get help if necessary.

Fear body language is all about escape. Your internal organs get geared up for you to run away: your heart rate speeds up, your blood-pressure rises, your liver floods your body with sugar. These preparations give you energy in order to flee – and also give you the classic symptoms of butterflies in your stomach as adrenalin surges, a cold feeling as blood rushes to support your internal organs, a dry mouth from rapid breathing, sometimes an urgent desire to go to the loo as if to lighten your body for faster movement! These internal signals are your body's way of telling you that there is something happening that you ought to run away from.

In fact, in most normal situations you stand your ground. You do not run away from a job interview, an argument with a friend or a tricky tackle on the sports field. You register the fear but ignore it and carry on regardless because, in reality, these are situations in which you want to succeed. And while you may turn rather pale, shake with nerves or lick your lips to prevent a dry mouth, you will show these responses in such a toned-down way that other people may not even notice them.

There is, however, one common situation in today's world where you not only feel terrified but show all the signals of real panic: horror videos. If, on screen, the door creaks open or the mad axeman strikes, your body reacts almost as it would if these events were really happening. You scream (to summon help), cling on to a friend (for support), flinch away (to protect yourself), kick your feet (as if to run away). Then you collapse in giggles as the adverts come on!

In fact, nowadays, when physical threat is rarely part of day-to-day life, your body may actually enjoy all this. In a strange sort of way, in a situation where you know that you are actually quite safe, giving your body such a thorough internal workout often feels good. Dracula and Frankenstein – thank you!

What Really Happens When I Am Angry – and How Should I Handle That?

When you get angry, you are getting ready to fight. Anger is what is left of the impulse that primitive humans had to attack whomever or whatever seemed to be a threat. So if a friend insults you or you get caught in a traffic jam, your body goes on full alert for the possible battle to come!

On the outside, your body will automatically take on a posture designed to warn off the attacker. So your shoulders may square as if for action, your head and lips may jut forward threateningly, your eyebrows may lower in the aggressive expression that monkeys use as a prelude to attack. And on the inside, your nervous, cardiac, circulatory and respiratory systems gear up for emergency action. What you feel on the inside, as this happens, may well be a rush of energy, an urgent desire to move, to hit out, to attack.

Of course, you will hardly ever really attack. Few situations nowadays lead to a full-scale battle, and it is rarely acceptable to come to blows, however irritated or frustrated you get. So you will try to stifle the anger, push it down and carry on as if nothing has happened.

This sounds good, but it has its drawbacks. Feeling angry is your body's way of telling you to take action – and if you cannot do that then your body is left high and dry, with all its

80

systems ready to act but not acting. The results can, in medical terms, be unfortunate; your body's responses may lead to diseases such as stomach ulcers, heart attack, depression. So while it is socially harmful to act on your anger, it may be physiologically harmful to your body to ignore that anger completely.

So if you feel angry, first note it. Then try to take the edge off your rage so you do not hit out. Take action – in any harmless way you can. Some people opt for slamming doors and banging down cups – but, more constructively, you could dig the garden, beat some rugs, play a hard game of squash. Clearing your body of the stress of anger will not only help you feel better, it will also make you better able to go back and tackle the problem that made you angry in the first place.

How Do I Use Body Language to Feel Better?

Something bad happens – a chance unkind comment or a real frustration. And though you can cope you are in need of a little comfort. How does your body help?

The first thing you will probably do is instinctively touch yourself. There is sense in this; being touched was the basic way that you were reassured when young. The most usual comfort touches are on the head and hands – where adults pat young children – and so your hand will move to your face, you may lean your cheek on your palm, stroke one

hand with the other, or pinch the fleshy part of your thumb.

Or your body may want the comfort of rhythm – another early reassurance signal. So you may 'rock', swaying backwards and forwards in a rhythmic movement that recreates being in the womb or being rocked in someone's arms. You may drum your fingers or feet in a way that imitates the sound of a comforting heartbeat.

You may also try to get comfort from others. Unconsciously your posture may slump, your head may droop and your gestures may become slow and weary almost as if you are so tired that you need to be carried. Your face shape may actually change, so that within minutes it becomes pinched and thin, or puffy and tired – childhood signs of needing to sleep

that in adults signal that they need to be
looked after. There is nothing actually wrong
with you physically, but your body sends out
these signs as the best way it knows to get
others to give it some attention and support.

What if there is no help around? You are in
public, at work, or in a situation where asking
for support just is not possible. Or you realize
that the best way to solve the situation is
simply to act. Then perhaps you will try to
cope, deliberately manipulating your
physiology to cheer yourself up. You may
straighten your posture – which makes it less
likely that you will feel sad. You may breathe
deeply in and out, which will relax you. You
may tip your head back and look upwards
– because this tends to distract your mind
from any distressing inner sensations. You
may start to move, shaking hands and feet or

shifting your body position – aiming to boost your energy to override your bad feeling.

At some point you may try to give yourself the comfort that other people are not giving you. Where possible you reach for a warm sweater, soft blanket or duvet; raising your body temperature helps you feel better because it releases energy that your body would otherwise use trying to keep your vulnerable internal organs warm. You may eat or drink warm, soothing, carbohydrate-filled meals – not only because warm food helps your body fight off fatigue and illness, not only because carbohydrates act as natural sedatives, but also because eating and drinking are part of your body's earliest memories of comfort.

Finally, you will probably opt for a good night's sleep. Sleep heals – so much so that, as described above, the natural response to feeling bad is often to become drowsy. And, given the chance to recover and refresh yourself completely, most things will seem better in the morning.

Is There a Way to Motivate Myself through Body Language?

What happens when you do not feel motivated to do something? It is not that you do not want to do it, nor that you cannot do it. But whenever you try, you get a sinking feeling in your stomach, almost a revulsion. You may feel irritated, so tighten your jaw and tense your shoulders. You may feel simply exhausted, with drooping eyelids and a heaviness in your chest.

From the outside, the body signals will be clear. You may sit heavily in your chair, with no muscle tension. Your eyes may be glazed, your head sunk into your shoulders. You may have your arms crossed in front of your body, as if to create a distance between you and whatever it is you are not motivated to do. Recent research shows that people who are uninterested in what they are hearing often display two clear and consistent nonverbal signals: they lean back and away from the source of what they do not want to hear, and they stretch out their legs in front of them.

Of course, the answer to such clear signs of demotivation may have nothing to do with body language. Perhaps you have been told to get on with a job you feel does not need doing; perhaps you have done the job so often that you are bored; perhaps you fear that you are going to get it wrong. If so, then you probably need to use words to figure out, alone or with other people, how you can think and feel differently about what needs to be done.

But if you simply want to feel more enthusiastic about something, then body language *can* help. The secret is that if your body behaves in a particular way, this often convinces your mind to follow suit. So remember how your body responds when you do feel motivated to do something. Maybe you feel more energetic: your posture may be more upright, your eyes wide open to see better, your head tilted to hear better. If seated, you almost certainly reverse the two key 'demotivation signals' and lean forward, with your legs tucked under you. You move quickly and alertly, to get on with the job. Inside, you feel neither queasy nor weary, but full of vitality, with a kind of 'buzz'.

Once you have identified the body language
that you personally use when you are
motivated, you need to alter your body
language deliberately to that pattern. You will
first need to raise your energy level, increasing
your heart rate and breathing – because
energy is the key to getting your body to feel
more positive about the job in hand. You
might want to take a short bout of exercise,
jumping up and down a few times or running
on the spot. Then, once you feel more
energetic, allow the rest of your body
language to take on a motivated pattern,
sitting up, leaning forward, tucking your legs
underneath you, opening your eyes slightly
wider, moving more quickly.

It may seem as if you are pretending to feel
something you don't. But if you use your
actions as a kind of 'pump primer' to get your

body going, pretty soon you will feel better about the job in hand, and spontaneously you will be better able to feel naturally motivated about it.

What Stages Does My Body Go through When I Am Grieving – and What Happens If I Ignore these Stages?

When you suffer a major loss your body grieves. It responds with a whole series of prolonged nonverbal reactions – but why? These reactions certainly do not bring back the person, relationship or job that you have lost. Instead, your body's responses almost seem to make things worse, incapacitating you as you cry, feel tired, get depressed.

But these body reactions are there for a reason. It is almost as if, having suffered a loss that you actually cannot do anything about, rather than trying to take action your body is

demanding extra support and comfort to
make up for that loss. The fact that you are
incapacitated forces you to give yourself that
extra support, or to allow other people to give
it to you, in a way that simply would not
happen if you were not feeling so bad.

The initial stage you may go through is shock.
Even if for just a few moments or hours, when
you first learn that you have suffered a loss
you become slightly numb, as if to protect
your body from the stress that will follow
when you fully realize what has happened.
Then, for a few days or weeks you may go
through a phase of being physically
vulnerable; getting tired easily, feeling dizzy,
suffering from minor illness, loss of appetite
or an inability to sleep. These reactions may
immobilize you, giving you an excuse to be
looked after.

In
memory
of
FLUFFIE
the best
budgie
in the
world

The classic sign of grief is that you cry
– although how much you do, and whether in
public or private, is likely to depend on what
gender you are and your cultural background.
But controlling yourself too much can be
unwise; tears are the body's way of reducing
stress, and contain substances that reduce
depression. It may seem 'weak' to weep, but
physiologically it is helpful; afterwards your
body will be a little better able to cope.

As time passes you may find yourself feeling
angry. You may feel angry at the event that
caused your loss, at the people responsible,
sometimes at whomever or whatever it is that
you have lost. This anger is a positive thing;
the effect on your body is to give you more
energy, making it possible for you to start
getting on with your life.

It is tempting to ignore the stages of grief. And, in fact, you may not need to go through every phase. But if you just carry on regardless when your body signals any of these stages, then full recovery is less possible. For the physical impact of loss is very real; studies have shown that following the death of a partner, for example, survivors are less able to fight off illness, more prone to develop cancer, more likely to die of heart disease. So pay attention to what your body needs when you are mourning. For grief can kill; dying of 'a broken heart' is no myth.

What Does My Body Language Tell Other People About My Personality?

The vast majority of your body language does not tell people anything about your personality – even if they think it does.

Some theories of physiognomy hold that your natural appearance – the shape of your face, the colour of your eyes – holds the key to understanding you. But in fact these characteristics are genetically inherited, not formed by your personality at all.

Also, a great deal of body language is flexible and variable, according to the context and your mood. So although it can be used to interpret what you are thinking or feeling at a single point in time, it cannot be used to analyse your underlying character, your baseline intelligence, or what kind of temper tantrums you consistently throw on a bad day!

So where does your body language reveal your personality? The answer is in those parts of your nonverbal appearance that have been formed by past and repeated life experiences. Some schools of psychology hold that by as young as nine or ten years of age, human beings have postures and expressions that are personal and which will get more fixed with age. If you constantly think a particular way, therefore, your face may take on certain lines; if you regularly feel in a particular way, your body will automatically drop back into a posture typical of that feeling.

To take an example, other people may be able to tell whether you are usually a contented kind of person or not. If you smile often, other people may notice 'smile lines' between the corners of your lips and the corners of your nose. These 'nasolabial folds' are stronger in the happier individual, and are often accompanied by a slight but permanent upward tilt to the corners of the mouth; you will probably also hold yourself upright and have relaxed muscles, particularly around the shoulders.

Say, on the other hand, you are a pessimistic type of individual. You may develop that permanent stoop, neck thrust forward, that gives the condition of 'depression' its name. Your nasolabial folds will be almost unnoticeable, there will be a slight but marked downward tilt to the corners of your mouth,

and you will have frownlines on your
forehead.

You cannot really hide such deeply etched
characteristics. But you may be able to change
them by slightly altering your body language.
If, for example, you make a habit of sitting up
straighter, frowning less often and smiling
more, then the signals you send out will
eventually be different and people will judge
you differently. And, responding to that, of
course, you may also end up feeling more
positive about life – simply because your body
language is more positive.

How Do I Know How Close to Be to Other People?

Just how close you want to be to people depends on how safe you feel with them. Unless we are in a crowd and have no option, we tend to keep people we do not know outside the 'public zone' of more than 3.6 m (12 ft). People we know only as colleagues or acquaintances can come within our 'social zone' of 3.6 – 1.2 m (12 – 4 ft) – though they may come closer to say hello or goodbye. Within the personal zone of 1.2 m – 45 cm (4 ft – 18 in), we allow family and friends, and only lovers and children are allowed to come closer than 45 cm (18 in), to cuddle up and actually touch.

But these distances are generalized. How close you want to be to others also depends on many other things. It can depend on how you were brought up: those raised in 'touching' families tend to grow up as touchers themselves. It can depend on the sort of culture you come from: one study revealed that in Puerto Rico acquaintances spending an hour together touched 180 times, while the score in Paris was 110 times, in Florida once and in London not at all! How happy you are to be close can even depend on how acceptable the other person's odour is to you: if he (or she) smells threatening, perhaps because his personal hygiene is poor, then you will unconsciously move back out of range.

How close you get also depends on the mood you are in. If you are upset you may well allow people to come very close and touch you for support. If you are scared, you will pull back from those you are wary of and keep extra close to those you feel can take care of you. At the other end of the extreme, if you are irritated you may keep well away from people so that they do not notice your negative expression or gestures – or so that you do not give way to temptation and lash out at them.

If other people get too close for comfort, your body sounds the alarm bells. You feel strong and often painful inner sensations, a combination of fear and anger that alerts you to danger and then tells you either to run or attack. So you may feel panic in your stomach or a rush of nervous energy that makes you want to protect yourself. You move back, turn away sharply and use angled gestures so that others have to step back – or you may even unconsciously frown and look angry so that people feel wary of you and spontaneously steer clear.

If, on the other hand, you feel you are too far away from someone, then you may also feel bad. If a friend chooses to sit on the opposite side of the room, or a lover chooses to sit at the opposite end of the sofa, you may feel uncomfortable and rejected. You will automatically try to cut down the distance between you – shifting forward, leaning forward or stretching out your hand to bridge the gap.

In body language terms, we spend a great deal of our lives dancing round people. We move forward, edge back, shift sideways, all to get just the right distance between us. Only when we get that balance of closeness and separation can we settle down and concentrate on interacting happily, person to person.

How Can I Develop My Leadership Potential?

Whatever the situation – guiding a group of friends to a restaurant or taking a sports team to victory – leading a group is more challenging than simply interacting one-to-one. You need to adopt strong and effective body language or you will not believe in yourself and the group will not believe in you.

So first, be aware of the body language of leadership. Good leaders seem confident; they use the nonverbal signs of self-assurance such as a 'head up' posture, directive gestures and sure movements. They look directly at other people rather than using the 'down and away' glance of a nervous follower. They do not necessarily shout – in fact if they do they often lose authority rather than gain it – but when they speak, other people listen.

Above and beyond these cues, which simply signal that you are a leader, you then have to involve the people you are with in what you are doing. When you explain things, you need to look round at everyone, making eye contact to draw them all in. Your gestures need to be 'inclusive' – open and towards your body – rather than 'exclusive' – closed and away from your body. And you need to spot anyone whose body language indicates that she (or he) does not feel part of the group, and make a special effort to invite her in, with a questioning look and a smile of welcome.

It can be crucial to control who is speaking
and who isn't. If you are using your nonverbal
skills correctly, then you will notice who
wants to talk because she will raise a finger,
lean forward slightly or take an inbreath, in
preparation to speak. You will then indicate
that you have registered that person by a
glance and a nod, and hand over to her when
there is a relevant pause. On the other hand, if
someone tries to butt in your direct glance
should give that person the message that she
should wait her turn.

It is also vital to be able to spot opposition
– and cope with it well. You may notice
someone with folded arms, an irritated
expression or a loud, sharp tone of voice and,
if so, you may want to allow that person to
express her view. But do not be afraid, as
leader, to overrule her, as long as you do it

confidently. Studies have shown that most leadership disputes are settled in favour not of the person who argues most convincingly, but in favour of the one who states her case with the most confident body language.

Lastly, you will need to know when the group is really 'behind' you – that is, the point at which you know you have succeeded as a leader. If you notice people looking down, turning slightly away from you or fidgeting noticeably, then you probably have not got full support. If you receive direct eye contact and noticeable nods of agreement, then relax. They are on your side.

How Does My Body Take Time Out When It Needs It?

Like any machine, your body cannot run nonstop. If you have a computer you will know that you regularly have to stop using it so that it can briefly save and process the information you have input. In the same way, brains need time to integrate what they have experienced.

In order to do this, as you work and play you spontaneously take regular 'time out' breaks to process what you are experiencing. If you catch yourself thinking through a problem by looking off into the distance or defocusing, then you are probably taking one of these breaks, even if only for a few seconds.

But you also need long breaks. You need more extended time away from stimulation and input. The ultimate break, of course, is sleep, when you take such a noticeable pause that your body shuts out everything, with closed eyes, 'deaf ears', and hardly any movement at all. But when you are not weary enough for sleep you may still need time without stimulation – when you are emotionally stressed, when you need to solve a problem, when you want to think things through. As the most physically arousing thing that a human being can see or hear is another human being, then this means time alone.

Your body's first line of defence when you feel like this is to try to reduce the stimulation naturally, by its own efforts. You may turn or look away, as you may feel unable to maintain eye contact without feeling bad, as if it is just not appropriate for you to be looking at other people. You may find that your normal range of hearing is lessened, as if it just is not appropriate for you to be listening to other people.

If these natural efforts do not work on their own, then your body may signal to you that more dramatic action is needed. It may make you actually feel uncomfortable until you take time out. You may feel tension in your back or jaw, a headache behind your eyes, or a feeling of nausea in your stomach.

And though you may not be aware of it, this discomfort eventually reveals itself on the outside. Your body language tells other people to go away. First, you signal that you are withdrawing from interaction. You become very still, you reduce all gestures, you 'blank out' your facial expression, lower your eyelids, make your voice flat and monotonous. The other person – not getting the lively response he (or she) needs in order to feel appreciated – instinctively cuts down on the interaction, leaving longer pauses between sentences, looking away from you more, eventually falling silent.

Then, if this does not work – because you are surrounded by people, perhaps in the office, on the train, at home – you start to signal more strongly. You develop angular movements, a frown, a jutting mouth; you may shake your head just slightly in a 'no' signal, speak in a sharp, aggressive tone of voice, use abrupt gestures. Without realizing it your body actually signals hostility, in a subconscious effort to force other people to go away.

Pay attention to all these signals. They are your body's way of letting you know that you are on overload. Next time you feel them, retreat to a quiet room with a good book or your favourite video. Staying on good terms with other people may well depend on being prepared to take some time out for yourself.

Can Body Language Help Me to Be More Creative?

You want to be creative – but you are stuck. What is happening? Your mind, instead of first accepting every thought that it has and then choosing the best from a large range, is saying 'no' to every idea. In the end nothing seems right and nothing seems to work.

There are many mental approaches to removing such creative blocks, and many of these approaches are useful. But because your mind is so influenced by your body – and because there are definite body language patterns both to being creative and to being

'blocked' – you can also try experimenting with your nonverbal approach and see if that helps.

People in a creative mood, for example, often display very particular body language patterns. They move easily, their gestures are often 'big' and 'wide', their eye movements sweeping and broad as if to see lots of things. They will take up space as they move, look and gesticulate this way and that. Their expressions are happy and content, in the excitement of being creative.

On the other hand, people who are feeling blocked creatively often display body language patterns that are very different. They sit rigidly, hardly moving, perhaps focused on one point ahead of them, perhaps looking down at the problem they are trying to solve.

When they move they do so hesitantly, perhaps beginning to make gestures, then stopping, shaking their heads and falling still and silent again. Their facial expressions are stressed and unhappy, because every thought they have seems wrong.

The key to changing your uncreative body language to a more creative one is to experiment with all the nonverbal aspects of what you are doing, to find one that allows your body language to become more free and less controlled. Try first of all to alter your environment. Change rooms, find a bigger space, go outside to work. Play music – or stop playing music. Change chairs, to a softer, harder, higher or lower one. Find a bigger table to work on, use larger paper, use different coloured pens.

Alter your posture: lie down, sit up, walk about. Try an uncommon position, such as sitting with your legs crossed; this will distract you from your usual way of thinking by changing your usual way of moving. Use bigger gestures, spreading yourself out across your workspace.

Rather than focusing desperately on the problem in hand, literally look around. Stare out of the window, stare at the ceiling, try going to a higher spot where you can see further. Get a different view of things.

Sooner or later, if you keep experimenting you will find a way of working that succeeds. By freeing up your body you will learn to free up your mind as well.

What Is Stress
– and What Can I Do About It?

Stress is increasingly common nowadays. It happens when an inappropriate number of demands are put on your body, without your being able to stop them. So on a physical level, experimental subjects who had to work hard in 38°C (100°F) heat became tense and anti-social. On a more emotional level, subjects asked to cope with unrealistic work deadlines week after week start to suffer the same symptoms.

Interestingly, it can be as stressful to have too little to do as to have too much, because somehow your body gets as frustrated by being under-used as it does by being overstretched.

What happens when you are stressed? When demands are put on your body, chemicals are released into the bloodstream. That is appropriate – once in a while. But if it happens too often, then these chemicals are released into the body at damaging levels, overstimulating all your vital organs and causing all kinds of problems. You may sleep much more or much less, eat much more or much less, gain more or less weight. You may feel constantly irritable, anxious or sad. Your immune system will be worn down by the constant demands on your body – so you may get more colds, more allergies, more skin problems – or worse.

In order to handle stress, you have to mount a two-pronged attack: long-term coping strategies and emergency measures.

Long term, you first have to put a stop to the demands being made on you. If you are in a turbulent relationship, perhaps go to a marriage guidance counsellor. If your job is boring, negotiate for different work conditions.

Then, to help your body cope with day-to-day problems, you should support it physically. A diet low in fat, salt and sugar but high in refined carbohydrates will build health. Less than 21 (for women 14) units of alcohol a week will make sure that your vital organs are not stressed by processing too much. Regular exercise will burn off the chemicals released when you get tense. And regular breaks from work or upsetting family situations will give your body a chance to recuperate.

Also, develop emergency measures to help you cope at the moment stress hits. As you become aware of your stomach churning and your tension rising, take a deep breath. Then let it out gradually, relaxing as you do, to a count of one through ten. Repeat this several times, until you feel yourself beginning to unwind. Make this simple relaxation routine part of your everyday existence; it will make you happier, increase your effectiveness – and help you live longer!

How Can I Build My Self-confidence?

In body language terms, confidence is the physiological proof that you feel able to do what you are about to do. Lack of confidence, on the other hand, is the opposite; it is your body's way of signalling that you are not able to go ahead – and that you really shouldn't be trying to.

Your body signals confidence not only to other people but also to yourself. The signs of lack of confidence are very similar to those of uncertainty and fear – because you are unsure of your capability, and nervous about that.

Your gestures will be jerky and uncoordinated;
you will show a lack of balance in the way you
sit or stand; you will shift position uneasily;
you will hesitate or stammer; your stomach
may churn and your mouth may go dry.

Recent work in the U.S. in the field of sports
psychology suggests that it is possible to teach
athletes to be more effective by having them
adopt the body language of confidence. And
there is no reason to suppose that most things
you attempt will not benefit from this approach.
This will not work if you simply cannot do what
you are trying to do; but if you are capable, and
are simply held back by lack of self-belief, then
using confident body language may give you the
extra physiological boost you need.

To try this, first prepare. Think back to a time
when you really were confident, perhaps during

your best performance to date. Make sure that your body is firmly balanced, bending your knees slightly if you are standing, placing yourself squarely on the chair if seated. Keep your spine straight and avoid any side-to-side wobbles. Let go of any signs of tension in your body: drop your shoulders; raise your head and hold it square and facing forward; breathe deeply; smile just slightly, which will also relax you. Check, once again, that your body is centrally balanced and as symmetrical as it can be without tension.

As you do, recall clearly that time you were confident. Take a moment to let the memory really build your confident posture. Use all your body language knowledge and skills to fill your body with enthusiasm and self-belief.

Then, go for it!